I SEE THROUGH MUDDY WATER

Signs of DOWN LOW Men

Nichol Collins

I See Through Muddy Water: Signs of Down Low Men

Manufactured in the United States of America

www.globeshakers.com online store and contact info

ISBN 978-0-9997545-3-5

Names have been changed to use discretion.

Visit www.globeshakers.com

Discount Bulk orders available

Table of Contents

My Other Books
Amazon links are on my Website (also Publishing Co)
https://globeshakers.com/pages/authors-corner

-Behind Enemy Lines (autobiography)

-I See Through Muddy Water (Signs of Down Low Men)

-Power: The Benefits of Tongues

-Church Politics Vol. 1-4

-The Fullness of the New Birth: Evangelism & Deliverance Manual

-Under Construction: Mens LGBT Manual

-No Residue: Women's LGBT Manual

-Effective Evangelism: Reaching the LGBT

-Walking in Power 30 Day Devotional

-Attributes of Jesus 30 Day Devotional

Yevette Fisher (My Mom)

-Devil Let My Baby Go
-Momma's Last Breath
-What About Conrad
-Holy Toledo
-No One is Exempt
-Walk by Faith Prayer Journal
-In Between Trains

I See Through Muddy Water: Signs of DL Men

FOREWORD

I highly recommend, “I See Through Muddy Water.” This story is on target, and very informative. It took courage for Evangelist Nichol Collins to expose her past sins to help others. I admire her sharing these facets of her testimony. I can personally relate to this story because I lived on the “down low” for years. This information being disclosed will leave you speechless. The down low lifestyle is stressful. Portraying a false image is tormenting, but the dishonesty is unfair to women.

In my past life I was a truck driver by day, and male stripper by night. I had a lustful appetite that would allow money to entice me into anything. I left the club one night with two women that I discovered later in the bedroom were transgender women. I still engaged in sexual encounters with them. After that incident I was "turned out," but embarrassed to come out the closet. I got on the internet to find more hook-ups with strange flesh.

I was in a terrible accident causing my 18-wheeler truck to go over a 100-foot cliff. I was found unresponsive. Once awakening from a combative coma for ten days, I saw the need to forsake my perverted lifestyle. I am now delivered through my obedience to Acts 2:38 and fasting regularly. I am happily married with children, serving the Lord, and have accepted my call to ministry. I know this "down low spirit" is very common and women can be so naive ignoring the signs. After reading this book you should be enlightened and able to identify this deceptive behavior.
-Chris Holmes

IN A NUTSHELL

At the age of seventeen, I chose to embrace a gay lifestyle shortly after graduating from high school a year early. After 3 months of exposure to the culture, I cut off all my long hair. I bound down my breasts and bought a whole new men's wardrobe. I passed for a teenage boy easily in society. My transformation was drastic like night and day. I dropped out of college and started selling marijuana, which eventually led to the distribution of several other illegal substances.

I was accepted by a close knit group of homosexual men that treated me like family. Two of them were transsexuals (biological men that lived as women with breast implants). I was the youngest in the bunch. This circle of friends taught me the flip side of this new culture. I adopted the gay lingo, which was a secret vocabulary used amongst the LGBT community. The term for heterosexual or Down Low men is called "trade." For example they might say, "Look at that fine piece of trade" or they might say, "my trade is coming over to see me."

Greed causes many to compromise their standards.

We hung out at an apartment Downtown L.A., smoking weed daily. I was baffled by the amount of DL (down low) men who came over. I discovered a lot of things about DL dudes early on. The gay guys and tranny's (transsexuals), were having sexual encounters with men who refused to admit they were bisexual. I recall many occasions that they locked up in the backroom together.

Some of these men that appeared to be "straight" were fathers, athletes, thugs, and regular everyday looking dudes. At that time, I thought all gay men wore lip gloss, switched when they walked, and had a flamboyant personality. I began to realize that a person's sexual preference had no image. Most people who live immorally want to satisfy their sensual desires **by any means** necessary.

Several straight men have been baited into homosexuality under the influence of drugs and alcohol. The predominant allurement has also been money in several instances. The bible says, "The love of money is the root of **all evil**." Gay men will go to extreme measures to get what they want and do not mind paying for sexual pleasure.

I "came out" onto the gay scene initially as a lesbian. After being around certain people within the LGBT+ community who seemed to do whatever was convenient, I ventured into other activities. I know firsthand that perversion has "no limitations." I knew girls who lived as boys who conceived with gay men, which is **hetero**sexual intercourse technically. There is no rule book and now more letters have been added on to the LGBT acronym as the years progressed.

Many effeminate gay men despised feminine women, but oddly they were attracted to my boyish illusion. Also, DL dudes were making advances at me since they had an inward yearning to be with a male. Sin has an insatiable appetite. I think we began to bond through trauma. Homosexuality is a manifestation of deeper issues such as: abandonment, rejection, abuse, low self esteem, and generational curses (Exo. 20:5, 34;7) which are typically the dysfunctions that lead many into alternative lifestyles.

My first time engaging in this type of activity was in Atlanta with a group of homosexual friends. We walked to Piedmont Park, which was a landmark for gay men to have sex in the woods. My mindset had been conditioned to pattern myself after a straight man, but after interacting with gay men over the years, I found myself conforming to their characteristics.

Ultimately, I entertained whomever showed interest as long as it benefited me in some form, and they were attractive. It was not necessarily an exchange of money for sex but they paid for everything like the drugs, alcohol, and hotel room. I had become fixated on using my strap-on dildo to penetrate both masculine and effeminate men (prosthetic penis in a harness attached to your body).

What took twenty minutes to get into, took me twenty years to come out of. I had no idea that sex, drugs, and rock n' roll would have led me nowhere. Satan never allows one to see the end result of what might be initially an experiment. I would advise anyone to be careful what you try once because you might become **addicted**. Perversion is likened unto a crack cocaine habit and will make you feel driven to routinely fulfill these sexual fetishes.

This book is to solely educate women. In my opinion, it is cowardly to live a **secret** life. I was always true to who I was as a sinner and made no attempt to hide it. Thankfully, God has changed my life around. Now, I have no problem exposing the devil's secrets. My life did a 180 in 2014 and

I can disclose these things to help someone else identify the **deceit**.

The names have been changed, but the stories are true and necessary to shed light on this subject. Some would take things I reveal to their grave, but as a minister I believe it is important to discuss real life scenarios amongst the church. I might not have used tons of bible verses, but this is still a transparent ministry tool. Women can have a tendency to think only prison inmates have potential to be DL, so I wanted to share five prototypes to dismantle this myth.

Men do not allow women to decide if they want to date a bi-sexual man. But instead women are lied to, misled, and their health is jeopardized.

I am no longer the guy I portrayed in the photo, but I have a story to tell from this era of my life. Buckle up for the ride !!

CELEBRITIES

I encountered celebrities from the time I was introduced to the LGBT lifestyle. The majority of my nights were spent partying in Hollywood, Ca. There was a designated area where gay people hung out. The donut shop on the corner of Santa Monica Blvd. and Highland was a high traffic area.

My hustler mentality began to expand as I sold everything from crack cocaine to ecstasy, and speed (methamphetamine). Transsexuals (biological men living as women abbreviated tranny's) prostituted on this strip from sundown to sunup. Most of the clients (dates/John's) were on some type of drug. Famous people discreetly cruised the back streets to pick up tranny's for sexual favors.

I witnessed these celebrities pull up to proposition tranny's. On occasions, I hopped in the backseat to sell drugs to them. Mainly, ecstasy pills were in demand. I remember my first crack (rock cocaine) sale to a thriving talk show host. He was so high, he was acting paranoid. He instructed me to leave the crack rock on top of the rear tire of his parked car.

A well-known actor featured in many films, and another mainstream rapper were regular clients on the transsexual prostitution stroll. The actor would take tranny's to a hotel and pay them a thousand dollars just to completely undress and paint their toenails. The NY rapper was a regular client of a thirteen-year-old teenage boy, nicknamed Lil Mama. This teenage drag queen was homeless because his mom was on drugs and he ran away from a foster home. Lil Mama started taking female hormones at around twelve years old and was referred to as "she." They were a high yellow complexion, with their own natural long hair flat-ironed. Lil Mama's stature was fishy, which is a gay lingo term for feminine.

For around two consecutive years this rapper would pass through "the bull" (street slang name for Santa Monica Blvd). He resided on the East Coast, but travelled to LA frequently at that time. Before Lil Mama passed away from AIDS, she claimed that they had unprotected sex the entire time they had been intimate. The rapper is still alive, but I always wondered if he had been infected with H.I.V. Rumors were circulating that a man named Dr. Sebi helped many in the industry with a herbal cure.

At nineteen, I was highly impressionable and susceptible to the culture. Just when I thought I had seen it all hanging around a group of gay boys/tranny's; the celebrities came out the woodwork's. In Hollywood, being bi-sexual seemed to be "the norm."

THE DIRTY COP

In my mid twenties, I dated an older woman named Taffy. I met her at an after hours and she started off buying drugs from me. Taffy was also bi-sexual. I was so skinny back then addicted to ecstasy pills and cocaine. My nickname was "Esko" like Willie Escobar, but I used a "k" because I was affiliated with the street gangs that were bloods.

I was in a relationship with Taffy for almost 8 years and we shared a place together. Many clouded decisions were made on drugs and alcohol and my loyalty to Taffy was toxic. We had physical altercations often, but because she was making $40 an hour and taking good care of me so I endured the chaos.

Our romantic life became very open. We bought men into our bedroom. I frequently used my dildo (prosthetic penis in a harness) to penetrate "so called" straight men. I used Taffy as bait. While these DL men were having sex with her, I would sandwich them from the rear. My actions would alarm her at times. Taffy feared that these men would react abruptly. But as I presumed, they went right along with the ambiance.

I had a keen eye to scout out these kinds of men. I could observe by the way they looked at me that they were down for the cause. With all the voluptuous, dainty women out in the streets you are interested in me looking like a dude? I thought to myself, 'That's a red flag because if you are attracted to a female who resembles a boy, then secretly you like boys.'

My girlfriend Taffy had a close friend named Nita that was a weird looking, tore up chick with a raggedy weave. Nita hardly ever looked decent because she spent all her money buying cocaine from me. She was infatuated with this guy. The first year that Nita dated him, we never met her mystery man.

Taffy received a phone call one-night inquiring about more cocaine for Nita and her boyfriend. They were too stoned (intoxicated) to drive. We got up and drove over to the location she provided. For the first time we met Nita's boyfriend named Tee. As Taffy and Nita sniffed a few lines of coke (powder cocaine) off the plate, Tee conversed with me.

“I don’t want to always have to go through Nita. Give me your number,” he whispered.

“Yeah man I understand,” I said, with my teeth clenched shut whispering my number.

Tee’s birthday came around a few months later. I remember the day Nita took off work early to prepare for their celebration. Her first stop was our house. She wanted to come and pick up an eight ball (3.5 grams) of coke (cocaine). Nita began to disclose that they were going to have a threesome for the first time.

“I been doing a prostate massage on Tee,” she said.

“Huh what’s that?” I asked.

“I put my hand inside his anal cavity and wiggle it,” Nita said.

“What in the world, that sounds gross,” Taffy said.

"Tonight, I'm going to let a tranny do the dirty work," she said, laughing.

On the evening of Tee's birthday, Nita called a tranny prostitute in the LA Xpress newspaper. Immediately after this threesome, Tee became distant toward Nita. She started visiting us daily, complaining about her estranged relationship and drowning her sorrows in drugs. Tee kept hanging out "alone" with the tranny from the birthday rendezvous night.

Tee and Nita both were cocaine addicts who worked in law enforcement. He decided to end his relationship with Nita to pursue the tranny named Sunshine. Tee's new interest was contingent upon payment, but he didn't care as long as his fetishes were satisfied. As a woman, you cannot compete with another man for your bisexual companion's attention.

Me and Taffy began operating an escort service on a small scale. Tee called me requesting more playmates. Nita and Taffy's friendship eventually ended behind an unpaid debt. We were happy to get rid of her since she was always lamenting over Tee.

Tee was on the Task Force that conducted drug raids. He was a "dirty cop" that went back to the crime scenes the following day to confiscate the criminal's belongings while the property was restricted with yellow tape. Tee had a garage full of stolen merchandise that he sold to people.

We were very discreet about this new Madame venture. Other men on the DL paid us a fee for our referrals. I started recruiting gay boys in on this operation who were **not** underage to accommodate clients (John's). I provided the drugs and transported the escorts to the client to pick up the funds.

Tee was a huge financial source that became compulsive on drugs. He wanted to get kinky while he was high. Since he was such a square (nerd), we charged him more money for services. He told us he had been in law enforcement for several years after dropping out of college. His awareness of urban culture was very little. He became corrupt by hanging with neighborhood thugs at a local bar. Tee was always claiming that he was from a prominent Crip Gang. He was very adamant about having sex with tranny's only, and found no interest in typical gay men. He was labeled as a "tranny chaser," (a man that is fascinated by transsexuals).

Tee was a person that had an excessive admiration for himself, defined as a narcissist. As a cop he felt he was above the law like an invincible super hero. This alter ego came off as grandiose and conceited, opposed to his sober personality of awkward shyness. He mastered how to project a false identity.

The tranny named Sunshine, that Tee was paying for sex became possessive. For use of a better term Sunshine was vindictive. She started bribing Tee for money without even fulfilling sexual favors. Then, Sunshine threatened to call the police station to report Tee's abuse of drugs, and solicitation of prostitution. This scenario was becoming super messy.

Eventually, they had a physical altercation high on cocaine and Tee was injured by Sunshine. His arm was broken by this big, tall transsexual. Tee had to go on a medical leave from his job claiming to have fallen off a motorcycle to his colleagues. The true story behind this injury was beyond shameful.

Now that Tee was temporarily off duty, his drug habit was spiraling out of control. The crazy thing is that while he was house-sitting for his mom during her one month vacation, he entertained Sunshine over there. That over bearing tranny started popping up later at Tee's mother's house when he could not be reached.

Tee had to rent motel rooms to avoid any further confusion. His elderly mother had no clue that Sunshine was biologically a man. He was avoiding his ex-girlfriend Nita, which knew where his house as a bachelor was located. As usual, misery loves company; Sunshine and Nita united as friends to stalk Tee together.

I was sending other tranny's to get paid from Tee. They complained about his weird fetishes. Some said the money was not even worth the headache of his bad hygiene and bizarre requests. I got paid as the middle man, so I encouraged them to keep the cash cow dispensing.

The thought of a transsexual looking like a woman possessing male genitalia is captivating to DL men.

Tee kept hinting around occasionally that he was attracted to me and Taffy since the night he met us. We would brush him off because we did not find anything attractive about him. He was short, chubby, and obnoxious. I perceive Tee thought he could persuade us into a recreational encounter without giving us any money. His cocky alter-ego led him to believe that he had enough charm to sleep with women for "free." He had an erroneous outlook on us because only money would persuade us to entertain him in a perverse manner.

In the wee hours one night, around 1 AM Tee called Taffy's phone. We both were awakened by the ring tone.

"Hi, Taffy would y'all like to make some money?" he asked.

"Of course, you know Esko keeps coke so how much you need?" Taffy replied.

"Let me talk to Esko right quick," he said.

Taffy rolled over to pass me the phone.

"Tee what's up what you need man?" I asked.

"Well a few things and hoping that you can help," Tee said.

"Alright shoot it at me," I said.

"Don't you have a strap-on?" Tee asked.

"Uh, yeah," I responded.

"How much can I give you to use it on me?" he asked.

"Hmm hold on a sec dude ok."

I muted the phone to tell Taffy.

"Girl this fool wants to pay me to plunge him," I said.

"Well you know he got money so don't sale yourself cheap," Taffy said.

"Ok let me see what he is willing to pay," I said.

"Hey, Tee I need $400," I said, without hesitation.

"Well ok, but wait ask Taffy will she join too," he said.

I relayed the message.

"What part do I play in this? I am not letting his fat butt on top of me," she whispered, disgusted.

"Tee what do you want Taffy for?" I asked.

"I want a prostate massage," he answered.

Taffy heard him on speaker phone. "Boy we need a thousand and the drugs will be included alright," she blurted out.

"Dang Taffy you're pushing it, but I will do $800," he agreed.

We immediately jumped up to get dressed, packaged some drugs in a sandwich bag, and tossed my strap-on dildo into Taffy's purse. Tee lived about 15 minutes across town with no traffic. He was living with a different female police officer that he was dating to steer clear of his stalking ex-girlfriend Nita and his tranny playmate Sunshine. Tee kept his drug addiction and homosexual fetishes concealed from this new woman. He hosted this orgy with us at his own newly built home that was furnished but vacant.

Upon our arrival he counted out 8 crispy one hundred-dollar bills. He was anxious to sniff pencil length lines of cocaine off a saucer through a 3 inch straw he cut. There was nothing moderate about his drug consumption. Me and Taffy indulged in a few lines of powder, but wanted to stay alert outside of our comfort zone. My mission was to do a job and get out of there after completing the mission.

Taffy took him into the bathroom to use an enema (saline laxative) on him. Gay men use this to clean out any feces from their rectum. This is a clear indication that an anal cavity is an **exit**, NOT an entrance. Taffy made sure he showered also since we had gotten complaints about his hygiene.

While Tee was preparing, I took my cargo pants and Timberland boots off. I fastened on my leather harness and dildo under my boxers while wearing a tank top. After Tee came out of the shower he wanted to begin with a prostate massage. We were clueless about how to do that.

"You got any gloves?" Taffy asked. "Not no surgical ones, but I own a pair of yellow kitchen gloves downstairs," Tee replied.

Taffy came back upstairs with one yellow rubber glove on, midway to her elbow. I had to refrain from laughing. Tee was laying there high and acting anxious. He instructed Taffy on how to insert her index and middle fingers gently into his anal cavity with lubrication gel. Then, as Tee got comfortable Taffy placed her entire hand inside of him. He said the prostate gland was what she was digging to fondle and it felt like a grape. I sat at the foot of the bed watching in disbelief. I thought to myself 'Ouch.'

Tee's large consumption of cocaine made him think he was reaching his sexual peak but he was not even able to get an erection. Now, it was my turn to use my strap on him. He wanted a pile of cocaine mixed in the lubricant to numb his insides. I had never been so disengaged, he was a complete "turn off."

We left after being over there about an hour and a half. I gladly split $800 with Taffy. Soon as we got halfway home, Tee called us back to offer us another $250 each. Out of greed we returned.

Tee's cell phone kept ringing this time around, but he sent the calls to voicemail. After the phone rang again for maybe the sixth time he finally answered. His speech was slurred and it was obvious he was intoxicated.

"Yeah what you keep callin' for?" Tee asked, in a rude tone.

I never heard what was said on the other end, but Tee was very nonchalant.

"Listen I'm out having a good time I will be home later," he said, ending the call.

"Hey man do that police chick you stay with got a key over here?" I asked, suspicious.

"Heck no that's her calling now. She thinks I'm out with my homeboys, but I practically live at her house. I would never give her a key over here," he said, assuredly.

Something in my gut didn't set right, but we continued. About thirty minutes later the alarm system went off. "Front door," the automated voice announced. Me and Taffy ran to the bathroom and locked ourselves in there. All I was wearing was my boxers, a dildo, socks, and a tank top. I was praying as my heart raced. A woman busted into the double doors of the master bedroom screaming.

"What are you doing up in here naked Tee?" she asked, shocked.

"What are you doing here at all," he yelled.

"Oh, really you are messing around with a man up in here?" she asked.

"A man.... ain't nobody got a man in here," Tee replied.

"You're a liar I see Timberland boots and you don't own a pair so what's going on?" she shouted.

All we heard was commotion as if she was attacking him. Taffy grabbed the back of the sceptic tank lid in her hand. We were spooked in that bathroom, hoping she didn't make her way toward our direction. I was so paranoid on cocaine, I contemplated going out on the roof through the window. The lady confronting Tee punched him, and from the sound of things he wrestled her to the ground.

The uninvited intruder finally left after Tee begged her to get out of his house. We exited out the bathroom quickly getting dressed. He was holding his mouth with a towel. Tee used crazy glue like an idiot to close the split on his lip.

Tee hit rock bottom on drugs. The scorned female officer who busted him in the act, reported him to the bureau. He lost his job after failing a drug test. We accepted the propositions a few more times at hotels in exchange for money. After losing his job on the police force, Tee started trying to lower the compensation. Eventually, we stopped hooking up with Tee.

MR. BLUE COLLAR

There was a dude named Donald that was a construction worker. My girlfriend Taffy had been long term acquaintances with him before we met and they had previous sexual encounters. Donald recently ended his relationship with his 'baby mama,' so he began to resurface back into Taffy's life. She told me that Donald allowed her to penetrate him with a strap-on dildo on many occasions.

Donald hinted around to me more than once that he was attracted to "studs" (urban term for girls that look like boys). I didn't find Donald attractive at all. He was short, medium build, with buck teeth, and a big nose. Taffy was the kind of woman that was an opportunist. She often made Donald bring us food, liquor, cigarettes, weed, etc. His proposal to have a "threesome" with us became annoying and persistent. I watched her engage with him once, but I had no desire to join without any money on the table.

Donald went to jail for some warrants, got assaulted while in custody, and his jaw was wired when he was released. He never wanted to discuss any details. It made me wonder if possibly this incident was a result of being raped by another inmate. When I asked it seemed to be a trigger for him and he was defensive.

Taffy's car was in the shop when Donald stopped by one night. He had no knowledge of our drug habit or sales. I had some customers calling me to deliver significant amounts of cocaine to them. Since we didn't want him in our business we were pondering on whether to ask for a ride. I was hoping that I didn't miss out on any money.

Taffy decided to squeeze some Visine eye drops in his alcoholic beverage. Donald passed out ten minutes later. He was like dead weight on the couch asleep. Taffy staged it to look like we all had sex. She unzipped his pants, left a tube of KY lubrication jelly opened, and sat a sex toy beside him.

We took Donald's car without his permission to run our errands. Taffy bought him back a bowl of soup from a Chinese carry out restaurant. She seemed to have used Visine to drug people before and was acting like it was no big deal. Taffy knew already he would awaken with a hangover. Since his jaw was wired, he could only drink liquids, which is why she returned with soup.

We took about 45 minutes to make our stops. Donald woke right up when we walked through the door. He seemed to be foggy about his surroundings. His expression looked puzzled.

“Did you slip me something?” Donald asked Taffy.

“Are you kidding me you wild tiger…You drank that pint of Hennessy on minimal ice and turned into a beast,” Taffy said, chuckling.

From my experience with Taffy she was a convincing liar. She would play mind games that could make you question your own instinct. Donald looked drowsy. Taffy kissed his forehead and suggested sleeping off his hangover a tad bit longer. After that day Donald never came back over. I am pretty sure he knew that he had been given something to knock him out. I bet he stopped being so trusting after that. From his previous stories of romantic involvement with studs, I could tell he was used to taking advantage of lesbians. I am sure after that night he would be more aware of his surroundings.

Strange fetishes become a noose around a person's neck.

A THUG

One occasion, after leaving a nightclub I stopped at a gas station around 2:30 AM. A dude in line while waiting to pay spoke. “Aye, how are you? My name is Ace do you ever go to any after hours?” he asked.

“Yea, I do my name is Esko” I replied. As we walked back to the gas pump he began to elaborate about his job as a shuttle driver for a weekly after-hours. It sounded interesting and I was always looking for new customers to sale drugs. We exchanged numbers and parted ways.

Ace lived in Watts, California in the Imperial Courts projects. The Jordan Downs, and Nickerson Garden were housing projects within the same proximity, which were identified by the paint color of the buildings. Through the years, I would pass through over there to hang out with a friend or two, but it was across town. After meeting Ace, I began visiting him in the projects more often.

We started off as "smoking buddies." We would hang out often to get high off marijuana, but I discovered later that he used cocaine too. Eventually, I mentioned Ace to Taffy, and she agreed to invite him over to her house for drinks. Once Taffy seen him, she was eager to have sex with him.

As Ace was engaging with Taffy, I sniffed a few lines of cocaine and my boldness increased. I was making eye contact with Taffy as she looked over Ace's shoulder. She saw me strapping up my harness and dildo. Taffy motioned 'no.'

I was determined to make this threesome official like a referee with a whistle. That was my always my goal to emasculate a guy by penetrating him. I had already felt the chemistry between me and Ace from us smoking weed alone. My intuition told me he would be ok with it.

As I eased up behind Ace, he never seemed suspicious of my presence behind him. “Whoa!” he said, upon the initial thrust. Taffy laid his head on her chest, and I proceeded to use my dildo positioned in a harness attached to my body. Once Ace left, Taffy was baffled about the outcome. She laughed so hard in disbelief. She expressed how nervous she was when I gestured that I was going to join in. She did not expect this “thug” to be on the DL. We kept Ace around for about 2 years as our playmate.

“Esko do you have your thing?” Ace asked, bashfully on occasions.

This became a routine each time that we connected. Sometimes my toy just fell in with no maneuvering. During those times I sensed that he had already been sexually active with a "man" the same day.

Ace was still my buddy after me and Taffy stop dating. He let me in on a secret after a while. Ace had a boyfriend who was also a gang member. They were both thugs from Watts that pretended in society to be (homeboys) friends.

It is common for two men to portray an innocent friendship, but privately engage in sex with each other.

GOD'S PLAN

For twelve years since 2002 I had been living in a residential neighborhood in the South Los Angeles region of California. The community called Leimert Park featured Spanish Colonial homes and tree-lined streets. My eight-unit apartment building sat on the corner of Stocker street and Mc Clung Drive. My living room window faced the busy main street Crenshaw Boulevard.

I was in the center of both historical and contemporary African-American art, music, and culture in Los Angeles. Everyone that I associated with knew where I lived because I sold drugs from the curbside of my home.

December 2014, the Lord turned my life around completely. I was tired of being on a twenty-year roller coaster ride of sin. My lifestyle of selling drugs, gang affiliation, alcoholism, transgender identity, immorality, and drug abuse had run its course. I got attacked from behind by a guy with a hammer and assaulted in the middle of the street. Miraculously, I suffered NO INJURY from that brutal assault. The devastation shook me up, but it also caused me to realize that **Jesus loved me.** I viewed this incident as a spiritual awakening that literally knocked some sense into me.

The following day, I returned on a Sunday morning to my childhood church of the Apostolic denomination. Jesus is the only one that could break the strongholds in my life! I was **chosen** to be an agent of change in the world. I was trying to figure out how to start a new life. The odds were against me, but God was orchestrating my footsteps.

After conversion, I immediately changed my phone number to avoid the temptation of fast money, and sexual pleasure. I bagged up all my drugs, paraphernalia, and sex toys. I discarded these items in the garbage dumpster across the street. My next endeavor was to move an hour away out of the inner city for a fresh start.

I had no idea which direction I was heading in. A lot of my time was spent in prayer and fasting. Dressing as a man for two decades was eventually going to shift as well. My biggest fear was evolving back into womanhood.

Leaving California was the furthest thing from my mind. I loved Los Angeles weather, and it was all I knew as home. On the contrary, I realized that I needed to at least get out of that toxic environment. The Lord used Bishop T.D. Jakes preaching on TV to say, "Make haste." This simple yet profound statement gave me goosebumps confirming that relocating was the best decision for my future. My mom had taken a leap of faith and moved to the Midwest two years prior.

The Spring of 2015, I sold my urban street wear and shoes to a consignment shop. I bought a plane ticket to reunite with my mother for a new beginning. I faced a long journey ahead of me to achieve my total deliverance. My hair was still low with deep waves, but I was no longer getting it cut at the barber shop.

I was going through the growing pains of allowing God to have dominion in my life. I disconnected from anything that reminded me of my past. I had not wore women's fashion in so long the thought of it gave me anxiety. I was afraid to explore the pathway ahead of me, but I was **willing and obedient.**

The next day my Life changed

UNHOLY APOSTLE

Coming to a new state was a refreshing transition. It was a blessing to be sober as I bonded with my mom. Our mother and daughter relationship reminded me of my teenage years. We started praying together, eating at restaurants, and shopping for my new women's wardrobe.

I was uncomfortable transitioning in the beginning, but I embraced biblical truths. My gender was assigned at birth, but the devil hijacked my identity for two decades. The more I fell in love with Jesus I began to love my femininity. Although I had not discovered a sense of fashion or perfected my appearance, I was joyous.

After residing with my mom for a year, I began teaching a bible study on an App called Periscope. Facebook didn't have the feature to stream live videos yet. I was able to share the word of God seen by live viewers, and they could type responses on the screen. It was very therapeutic being able to talk about my past on Periscope.

A man was joining the broadcast typing very encouraging remarks. I called my nightly bible study, "Burning the Midnight Oil." After this guy was supporting me for two weeks, I became curious to put a name with a face. His Periscope username was CJ Parker.

Most of my followers, at that time had ministry titles in front of their name to identify their clergy positions. After typing CJ Parker in the search on Facebook he came right up. We had some mutual friends in common on social media. His profile description stated that he was an Apostle. Immediately, I felt honored that he had been watching me teach on Periscope.

There was a flyer posted at the top of his Facebook page. It appeared he did some travelling to neighboring cities and states. Ironically, Apostle Parker was coming to my new city to preach the following month. I commented under the post that I was from Los Angeles, and just relocated to Ohio eight months ago.

Instead of conversing in an open forum under the flyer, I received a private inbox message from Apostle CJ Parker. His response was that him and his wife were just looking at my testimony last night, and it's such a coincidence I'm in Ohio. I thought to myself, 'Wow God is really working in mysterious ways.'

He invited my mother and I to meet him and his wife at the service in a few weeks. After viewing a video of him preaching I was excited to attend this revival. I told my mom about him contacting me, and she put the date on her kitchen calendar.

By the end of the week Apostle Parker messaged me again asking for my phone number. He said there was a word of prophecy he was led to share with me. He spoke with me and my mom together and told us some things we were praying about. He specifically mentioned a documentary would be filmed about my life in segments. There is no way he knew these things.

A few days later, a random woman contacted me through Facebook. She referred my testimony to an agency for filming. My story about being an EX transgender male who was dating women, selling drugs, and affiliated with gangs was very interesting to several people. This EX-Gay ministry scheduled to film my documentary in 2 months. I was shocked that Apostle Parker foretold this, and that it came to pass so quickly.

Within 2-weeks we would be meeting Apostle Parker in person. He began to call daily. Me and my mother enjoyed talking about the Lord with him. He had a lot of biblical knowledge.

"The Lord dealt with me again concerning you Nichol, but I will be 100% sure about it once we meet," he said.

"Oh, ok amen Apostle Parker," I said.

I continued to teach my "Burning the Midnight Oil," Periscope broadcast. Apostle Parker began calling after I got off the video late at night. My mom figured he was calling since we were all online minutes ago, but still wondered if that was appropriate.

I began to wake up to text messages from Apostle Parker that read "Good Morning Beautiful." I figured it was an innocent compliment. But by the third morning the Holy Spirit within me whispered, "That's inappropriate for a married man." I thought to myself naturally, 'Surely this Man of God is just trying to be encouraging; since he knows my testimony.' Also, his wife was a decent-looking woman, fashionable, and had a nice figure.

On the other hand, I felt weird in a wig, wearing hand-me-down clothes, and was battling low self-esteem. I was in my premature metamorphosis stages from Caterpillar to Butterfly. I certainly did not think that I was attractive to anyone. I wanted to give a Pastor the benefit of a doubt.

The weekend to meet Apostle CJ Parker finally arrived. We only had to travel within a 2-mile radius. The hosting church was a small store front building. It was about twenty people present at the revival. We were excited to be at church.

Apostle Parker was escorted into the service. He entered the room with such a confidence. He had a persona about him that made him stand out in the midst of everyone. The charismatic sermon was well executed. Towards the end, Apostle Parker acknowledged us.

“Can I share a snippet of your testimony?” he asked, looking at me over the pulpit. I nodded, ‘Yes.’ He told me to stand up as he proceeded to give a condensed introduction of how we crossed paths. Apostle Parker elaborated on the power of God to rescue me from the bonds of a LGBT lifestyle.

The host Pastor of the revival gave some closing remarks during the benediction. He referred to his kids working in the ministry with him as he pointed them out. His daughter was playing the drums and looked like a tomboy in a plaid button-down shirt, jeans, and tennis shoes. Then the Pastor's son, which escorted Apostle Parker into service had some feminine tendencies and appeared to be wearing powder concealer on his face. Immediately, I recognized the Pastor's kids were struggling with their sexual identity.

The Pastor explained why they had downsized into such a small building. "An ole stanky ho lied on me y'all, so I lost some members!" he said, bitterly. My mother and I were discreetly nudging one another. I was appalled that a preacher would use such tacky language in the house of God. That was my cue to never visit that ministry again.

Once the service dismissed, Apostle Parker approached us to introduce us to his wife that he called, “Lady P,” which was an abbreviation for Priscilla. They were both such pleasant and vibrant people. I thought to myself, ‘Aww they’re just the cutest couple.’ We took a few group photos together. Apostle Parker walked into the back and left us conversing with his wife for a moment.

He returned within minutes. “Honey I’m going to walk these ladies to their car,” Apostle CJ Parker said. We exited the building toward our vehicle parked within twenty feet. It was during the Spring, and the night breeze was refreshing after being in that small hot box.

“I’m so glad you ladies came out to meet me,” Apostle Parker said.

“I am too,” I replied.

He grabbed my hand and slid some folded-up money into it.

"The Lord told me to be a blessing to your ministry," he said.

"Really?" Mom said, grateful.

"Wow thank you," I replied.

He seemed like a hero flying in to save the day, we didn't have a dime at that time. As we stood at the car, he looked at me grinning.

"Listen Nichol you remember I told you when we met that I would know something for sure?" he asked.

"Oh yeah you did mention that," I said, puzzled.

A man pulled up and interrupted as he hopped out of his car in the middle of the street. He complimented Apostle Parker's red rope strings in his dress shoes and expressed how much he enjoyed the sermon. Another gentleman was approaching, which he knew already. We told him goodnight and got in our vehicle to head home.

The next day Apostle Parker called me. "Hi, Nichol how are you today?" he asked.

"I am blessed," I replied.

"That's wonderful I wanted to finish our conversation from last night because I never got to tell you what the Lord put in my Spirit," he said.

"Ok, but I really want to thank you again for that money. I appreciate it!" I said.

"Oh, don't worry about that. Listen though, the Lord told me there is a platform being prepared for you, and I am supposed to get you ready. Give me 90 days, and I will have you equipped to go anywhere in the world," he said.

"Wow, I feel so honored," I said.

I felt excited as my adrenaline rushed. I was new in my spiritual walk, but eager to be an instrument for the

Lord's work. It seemed to be a privilege that someone would take out the time for lil' ole me. Since Apostle Parker claimed, "The Lord said," it never crossed my mind to **pray** about it and seek the Lord for myself.

My mother and I began having bible study over the phone with Apostle Parker. He was giving me homework assignments and asking biblical questions to see what I already knew. This reminded me of when I was enrolled in bible college as a teenager. It seemed like this connection was truly God ordained.

"Just when I lost hope, God sent you to show me that he is still working miracles Nichol," Apostle CJ Parker exclaimed.

Apostle Parker and me seemed to talk more often now that we had met face to face. He called a few times throughout the day. He even would send messages to me on Facebook in between our conversations. My mother had begun to trust him because he seemed like an alright guy.

Apostle Parker would exegesis one scripture for an hour. This means he dissected the text for a critical explanation. I was responsible to email him term papers on biblical subjects. It was like having a personal instructor holding me accountable.

Things started changing swiftly after two weeks. Apostle Parker stopped talking about the scriptures. He became comfortable venting to me about his stressful life as a leader. I didn't think it to be strange initially to have a normal conversation outside of God. People always seemed to feel comfortable opening up to me in the past.

"In order for you to understand the value of my time and validity of my words, you must get to know me as a person," Apostle CJ Parker said.

"Oh ok," I said.

"It's important that we become acquainted as we build a covenant relationship," he exclaimed.

He began to give me a lot of compliments. "You're an attractive young lady. I can see you being married one day," he said.

At that point I wasn't thinking about marriage, I had just transitioned into a woman. The first thing people want to do with Ex-homosexuals is pair them off with the opposite sex. I desired a closer walk with the Lord more than anything. I did not want to be distracted by any counterfeits.

The more Apostle Parker flattered me, I gained confidence. I began to feel like he genuinely cared about me. Every morning he text me something nice, and always sent a message to say 'goodnight.' This was beginning to seem like a concerned leadership figure.

"You're such a breath of fresh air. It is so easy talking to you because you're not judgmental," he said.

"Awww thanks Apostle I try to be relatable," I said.

"I hope I'm not getting too personal, but what was it about being with a woman that you liked?" he asked.

"Well it is an emotional tie before anything because women are sensitive creatures. Then it evolves into sex, and the chemistry can be mistaken as normalcy," I replied.

I wasn't expecting him to ask that, but I certainly didn't want to seem immature or seem uncomfortable discussing this subject. Looking back in hindsight it was an awkward question from a married Pastor. He pried deeper in it. From that day forward that conversation gave **entry** to the devil's doorway. This man was subtly seducing me, and I didn't even realize it at the time. I was in a utopia thinking that all Christians were **good** people, especially a man of God.

"Watch out for false prophets. They come to you in sheep's clothing, but inwardly they are ferocious wolves."
—Matthew 7:15 (NIV)

One evening Apostle Parker text me to ask if I could find a dentist for veneers in his city. I thought to myself, 'Excuse me sir.' The next morning, he had the nerve to call to follow up if I had the information.

"Apostle with all respect why can't your wife find a dentist?" I asked.

It was silent for a moment.

"I really don't dump my issues on anyone or talk about this situation Nichol, but my wife is very sick," he said.

"Oh, wow sorry, Apostle Parker please forgive me," I replied.

"You have no idea what I'm going through. My wife is on more than five different medications, and she has a pacemaker," he expressed, sadly.

I was lost for words. My eyes teared up as I tried to hold back my emotions. I felt so bad for him as I listened to his pitiful voice.

"Oh no that's awful," I said, with my voice cracking.

"You know what they told me at her last Dr.'s appointment? The physician pulled me out the room and said don't be surprised if I wake up beside her and she is gone," he said.

"What… I am going to be praying for a miracle and tell my mom to agree for her healing," I said.

"Don't cry everything will be fine. I am prepared for it mentally because she took ill shortly after I married her. She is my second marriage and luckily, we have no kids together. I have 7 children by 4 other women. Life is tough, and that's why you are such an outlet for me to escape my overwhelming circumstances. I gotta get some things done, so we will chat later ok, bye," Apostle Parker said.

My mood was affected by this terrible news. Hearing that my mentor may lose his wife any day now was devastating. It seemed like our connection got stronger when he disclosed this information as a bond of trust. I had no idea what the fate of Lady P would be, but I was genuinely hoping that his wife received a miraculous healing.

My mom asked me when Apostle Parker was going to resume with our bible study. I did not have a clue when that would be. But I knew that he had definitely veered off track. It seemed like he was intrigued with my constant evolving naturally.

Apostle CJ Parker sent me a photo of an exotic woman with beautiful make up on. He told me in the text message, that's how he wanted me to look. He even started to coordinate a few of my outfits through video chat while I was out shopping. He and his stepson were clothing stylists and recently had launched a business together.

Apostle Parker developed a regular routine of adulation. I was beginning to develop a crush on this married man of God. I started condemning myself, feeling convicted in my Spirit, and oppressed with self-accusation. I was so confused about these ungodly feelings that sprung up, I prayed fervently for this to disappear.

I was naïve, seeming to have tossed all my "street sense" out the window. All along Apostle Parker had lured me in with flattery, which is a characteristic of a snake. It dawned on me that this "unholy Apostle" was trying to groom me to be the next first lady of his ministry. He wasn't even going to let his wife get in the grave first. He was using manipulation, and spiritually that is a form of witchcraft. That unfortunate news about his wife's condition was bait to justify his actions.

"Do you think you and your husband will perform oral sex with one another?" he asked, nonchalantly.

"I was taught growing up it's sodomy," I replied.

"I don't tell my congregation what is permitted in their bedroom because I am hitting all my wife's holes," Apostle Parker said.

I was baffled at that point; a red flag went up. I realized Apostle CJ Parker was on the "down low." A heterosexual man would not want to anally penetrate a woman. A woman's vagina was made to SATISFY a man and if that is not enough for him something is odd. It had already caught my attention that he had a flare with colors, prints, and busy socks. I was beginning to connect the dots. I was indecisive with mixed emotions contemplating if I should be offended or overlook the situation.

His wife, Lady P had a handsome son. I began to inquire about him, but Apostle Parker emphasized that his stepson would certainly cause me to backslide. He even used some profanity, so I knew he was upset with the whole idea. Apostle Parker was on a diabolical mission trying to drag me back into perversion for himself. It would not have surprised me if he was aiming for a threesome with his wife. Something was not adding up.

Apostle Parker and his stepson had similarities with their style of dress. They both were excessively groomed. Inwardly, I felt that the two of them were lovers. The stepson seemed to be a good catch, but he was single. And many of their photos were without Lady P. It was weird in my opinion.

I observed more bizarre actions from Apostle Parker. When I watched him teaching live on camera, he looked high on drugs. He was constantly sniffling as he solicited prayers for severe sinus problems. His horseplay over the phone was childish. "CJ do you drink?" I asked. Instead of a direct answer he belted into hysterical laughter. A man of God should have been appalled and given a sober minded response.

I had lost respect for him to the point that I was calling him CJ instead of his ministry title Apostle. I no longer felt the need to be respectful, and he had took me back almost where I started in habitual sin. I was beginning to feel disconnected from God and slipped up using profanity talking to him at times. His flirtation and unholy conversation were affecting my Spirit. The bible says in 1 Corinthians 15:33, "Evil communication corrupts good manners."

I was on a vacation filming my documentary in Chicago. Apostle Parker text me to ask for prayer from me and my mom. He said he had a torturing toothache that needed immediate medical attention. It was in the middle of the night, so he was debating going to the Emergency Room.

The following day Apostle Parker called me while I was still out of town. “Hey, how are you? Listen, I owe you an apology. My toothache was from the Lord whipping me for the foul things I been saying out of my mouth to you. I went down in my office basement to pray. God said, ‘He chose you to be a vessel of deliverance for Him, and I will not pervert his specimen of grace.’ I am sorry,” he said.

“Wow, God is really concerned about me. I feel special to the Lord,” I replied.

I thought he was sincere and could still be an asset to the building of my ministry. I watched him teach on Periscope a couple of nights out the week. I took a break from teaching my Periscope broadcast. I had some more soul searching to do. I felt so out of sync with God.

Around 2 AM I got a text message from Apostle Parker. It read, ‘Feel free to share anything on your heart.’ I got nervous. I was getting mixed signals about what he could be implying. Then it crossed my mind if this was his wife fishing for something. I had been praying all week for the attraction to be severed so that we could start back with the ministerial training.

I replied via text, ‘Thank you, but I’m not quite sure what you mean Apostle.’

‘Once again, I want you to know there is no judgement if you share anything on your hear it’s confidential,’ he responded.

‘Thanks goodnight,’ I typed as a reply.

The next day Apostle Parker, called from his car. He had some worldly music blasting and his tone sounded very urban; meaning like a dude off the street. His voice also sounded anxious.

"Hey Nichol, check this out alright let's cut the chase here because its chemistry between us. We can't keep acting like it ain't no elephant in the room. I got a thang for you, and I know you feelin' me so what's up?" he said, confidently assertive.

"Well in all honesty I would have never initiated a conversation as such because it's something I been praying for God to eliminate. I am very convicted and feeling a sense of guilt," I replied.

"No, don't beat yourself up, this is completely normal. I am going to get you ready for your husband. These are natural emotions that God placed there. I just felt we should expose the devil, so we can move forward with God's work," Apostle Parker insisted.

"Amen," I said, hesitantly.

I was speechless. I was not thinking he would have expressed all that so boldly. I discerned he had been subtly flirting, but to hear him flat-out address me was shocking. This man was sending me on an emotional roller coaster. I guess my response to him was not viewed as the best answer by mentioning "guilt." He reversed it quickly back to God, claiming we could do ministry now that the air was clear. This man was a cunning predatory groomer that was tactical with his approach.

I was relieved feeling like a weight lifted off me. Once again, I believed that he was going to follow through with the prophecy he gave me when he said, "The Lord told him to get me prepared for the Nations."

Three days later he called me on the video camera through Facebook Messenger. When I answered the call, Apostle Parker was standing in his bathroom naked masturbating. His nose was running, and his eyes were big as a deer in headlights. It was obvious he was high on drugs. I did not hang up and I am responsible of staring into the camera aroused by his actions. I was not spiritually grounded to rebuke him or deny my flesh of a live porn show. "I gotta go, my wife is waiting on me upstairs," he said, whispering. I quickly took a screenshot and emailed it to myself, so I could erase the photo from my phone.

That really messed my head up. I could not stop envisioning him in the nude. My instinct that I misjudged as over reacting when the morning text messages were initiated, was now confirmed. John 14:26 talks about the Holy Ghost will teach you all things. All the years I abused powder cocaine, I had suspicions that his sinus issues were drug related all along.

Apostle CJ called the next day laughing. "Nichol, I am sorry I cannot help myself," he said.

"Man, you're so double-minded. One-minute God said I'm his vessel, and he warned you. Then it gets worse each time you apologize," I said.

He quickly changed the subject.

"Listen! I'm having a revival at my church. I want you and your mother to come spend some time with us. I am going to cover the expenses. I want you to give your testimony. I'm going to call your mother and let her know," he said.

I had no idea how I was going to ease away from Apostle Parker. He was so conniving that sometimes him and his wife called to talk to my mom on Face Time. Like an idiot I sent some things myself that I am embarrassed of acting in FLESH. I was just coming out of a 20 year promiscuous lifestyle. Being freshly out of that environment for one year had not manifested an overnight deliverance. I was right back where I started in the sense of lust.

After being invited to their weekend revival, my mom was really looking forward to a 4th of July getaway. Our outings were limited in Ohio, so we were anticipating going elsewhere. I was nervous in a sense and hoping my mom would not discern things had gone in left field.

We had a great time on our road trip driving there. Apostle Parker had text while we were on the freeway. He asked me to make him aware of our arrival. He ended up briefly stopping by alone to greet us. He came up to the room to see my mom. I walked him to the elevator. "When you all get to church tonight, don't mention that I already saw you guys," he said. I nodded uneasily.

When I walked back into the hotel room to relay the message to my mom, she was shocked. "Oh, that's out of order. I thought that was strange that he came by here, and he seemed to be nervous," she said. I just remained silent hoping she didn't dwell on it. We barely had arrived, and Apostle Parker was already up to "no good."

We had enough time to take a nap, and shower for church. As we left out, it began to rain. We drove across town about twenty-five minutes on the expressway. As we approached our destination, we were looking for the church address. Once the automated voice announced we had arrived I'm thinking, 'I don't see any sign of a church, are we at the right place?' We slightly rolled down the car window to listen for music. I heard a faint jingle of a tambourine.

We walked into a small room that was filled with about a fifty people. Right away, I began wondering where was this beautiful sanctuary I saw on a Facebook video. Obviously, I watched a clip as a guest speaker at another church's revival.

A concession stand was in the rear corner selling beverages and snacks during service. People were eating at their seat like the movie theater. It was not the typical sacred environment that you feel at traditional churches. Apostle Parker was hosting this revival. His guest speaker, named Prophet Ramirez drove in from another state. Towards the closing of the service the guest speaker called out Apostle Parker's wife. "Lady P, please come to the front," Prophet Ramirez said, motioning. She got up and walked a few steps to stand before the audience.

"The Lord said that you and your husband have a unique ministry. Apostle Parker is called to mentor women, and you are to interact with men as a spiritual mother. Oh, and God says to tell you tonight that you shall live and not die!" Prophet Ramirez said, on the microphone.

Apostle Parker was playing the keyboard softly. But when this good news was given about his wife, he sat there with a blank stare. The piano keys spiraled into a dong, dong, dong, with a gloomy undertone. The stepson that I thought was attractive, happily leaped up in the air. Usually in charismatic churches, the organist would start playing up-tempo praise music to allow parishioners to rejoice.

Instead, the atmosphere felt like we were at a recital. I thought it was a convenient "false word of prophecy" to give Apostle Parker more liberty to talk to women without the suspicion from his wife.

After service Apostle Parker bought over some of his members to meet us and also Prophet Ramirez and his wife. It was still raining, so Apostle Parker suggested following him back to the freeway to show us a quicker route back to our hotel. He pulled up beside us in an older car that sounded like there were immediate repairs needed. I had seen him on Facebook posing on the hood of a Mercedes Benz in his Sunday's best ensemble. Visiting his church was shedding light on this social media facade that he was not who he was posting to be on digital platforms.

The following day, my mom went to fuel up our car for Sunday morning service the next day. While she was gone Apostle Parker called. We exchanged in casual conversation. “Hey church was good last night. God delivered good news about your wife’s healing. Were you in shock though because you showed no emotion?” I asked.

“Nichol to be honest, ‘Oh no not another year of this,’ I was thinking when Prophet Ramirez told my wife she wasn’t going to die,” Apostle Parker said, bursting into laughter.

This dude was a cold piece of work. His response was unexpected. Apostle Parker brushed off that subject quickly. He was becoming unpredictable. Surprisingly, he was acting like his marriage was more of a curse than a blessing.

“Well, I am excited to hear you share your testimony tomorrow. Get your rest and tell your mom I called to say hello ok… goodbye," he said.

We had a wonderful night's rest and arose for the church service in good spirits. I was nervous about standing in front of people to tell my story. This would be my first ministry-related speaking engagement. I was praying that the Lord would give me what to say and not freeze up. I already felt unworthy due to my previous inappropriate conversations with Apostle Parker. This was beginning to **weigh heavy** on my heart.

I had made a poster board display of before and after photos. I couldn't even afford a retractable stand then. To God be the glory he was merciful, I did a good job as a first-timer. Apparently, the group of people in attendance at the Friday night revival were visitors. At Sunday service, the crowd had dwindled down even smaller. There was only about twenty people present, so it kept me from having an unsettled stomach. My mom recorded it, and shared it on her social media page.

There was a lesbian girl dressed like a boy sitting in the congregation. After church was dismissed, I introduced myself to her. She was very encouraged to see the transformation that the Lord had performed in my life. We became Facebook friends, and it felt fulfilling to plant a seed in that one young lady's life.

My mom and I went back to the hotel to change our clothes to eat dinner. We discovered a Cheesecake Factory, which was a delight because we did not have one in our city. That was one of our favorite places to dine in Los Angeles. We were having a nice 4th of July weekend. However, I thought it was odd that Apostle Parker did not take us out to dinner as his out-of-town guests.

The holiday was that Monday. Apostle Parker called to invite us over to his house for the 4th of July to eat. "I got a surprise for you, but I better tell you ahead of time, so you can come prepared," he said, on the phone.

"Really what is it?," I asked, excited.

"I have a videographer coming to film the next segment of your documentary," Apostle Parker said.

"Wow! Apostle Parker thank you I better pick out something else to change into for this. What time should I be there…are you barbecuing?" I asked.

"One o'clock is fine and no we aren't cooking barbecue. I think my wife is baking some fish," he said.

"Oh, ok see we will see you later," I said.

We arrived at Apostle Parker's 4th of July indoor gathering. It was a total of 8 people there including my mom and me. The videographer pulled up at the same time as us. But we had no idea who she was until she came in with her equipment.

Apostle Parker stayed in a nicely decorated, older Victorian style home. It reminded me of the house I grew up in as a child. We all sat around their dining room table nibbling on appetizers. Prophet Ramirez's wife was pregnant, so she ate half the cheese and cracker tray. Lady P was dressed like June Cleaver with a pearl choker necklace, knit sweater, a long maxi skirt, and "stiletto high heels while cooking."

Apostle Parker and Prophet Ramirez went down in the basement. All six of us ladies were getting acquainted. Me and Mom are easy to get along with, so we all clicked. My mom and

Apostle Parker's mother really interacted well. They were drinking coffee and eating donuts as they waited on the food to be prepared.

The videographer and I decided to begin filming the documentary in the living room. There was a thick wooden sliding door to block out any background noise. The young lady hired for the filming project was autistic. She appeared to be very smart, but her voice sounded like "Kermit the Frog." It took about 50 minutes for me to share my testimony while she recorded. The food was ready by the time we finished filming.

Apostle Parker and Prophet Ramirez were summoned from down in the basement to come and eat. They sat at the table cracking jokes like two class clowns. They mocked the autistic girl by imitating her. Apostle Parker laughed so hard at her voice that he almost fell out his chair. "You guys act like you took communion down in the basement," my mom said, jokingly. They hit the glass table and laughed uncontrollably.

The food was delicious. Everyone was enjoying a pleasant holiday among each other. The fellowship was pleasant.

"Honey we don't have any dessert," Apostle Parker said to his wife.

"We sure don't, and I forgot when I bought groceries this morning," she replied.

He pulled out some money and handed it to her. Prophet Ramirez's pregnant wife was anxiously waiting on that apple pie and ice cream. My mom, Prophet Ramirez, his wife, and Apostle Parker's mom were all talking each other's ears off. The videographer fell asleep on the couch with her shoes kicked off. I got up to get a beverage out the kitchen.

"Let me show you my music studio in the basement," Apostle Parker said, as he walked up behind me.

"Ok sure," I said.

I walked down the cement steps into the basement. He lied, there was no music equipment down there. It appeared to be a premature project of a man cave. He walked me through, pointing out where the recording booth would be. He went behind his desk and grabbed a box of wine from under the table.

"Have a drink with me," Apostle Parker said.

He poured a tall over-sized cup about 24 ounces full. Immediately, I felt awkward.

"Nah, I better not my system is clean and I don't want my mom to smell alcohol on my breath," I said.

Apostle Parker gulped down a substantial amount of wine. He persistently handed me the cup. I guzzled down some and handed back the cup of wine. He grabbed me in a bear hug, kissed my neck, and started groping me.

I struggled to break loose from him. I was a little startled at his aggressive spontaneity. Just as I shoved him backwards, Prophet Ramirez was standing in the doorway. It happened so quickly, if nobody was upstairs he may have raped me. The impulse of his wife at the store for a moment had him making a desperate attempt for a quick sexual advancement.

“Nichol listen we are trying to hang out with you have some more to drink with us,” Apostle Parker said. Prophet Ramirez sat down looking sensual. I turned around and dashed up those basement steps. That whole scenario transpired down in the basement within ten minutes. Lady P hadn't even made her way back with the pie yet. I really was trying to adjust my countenance to avoid looking disturbed. The videographer was still asleep on their couch, and that was her first-time meeting everyone.

Prophet Ramirez and Apostle Parker came back up from the basement. Lady P had returned with the dessert. "Hey, Apostle Parker you got any hair gel or grease I can use on my hair before we go on Periscope?" Prophet Ramirez asked. They both locked up in the bathroom for about twenty minutes. It was the strangest thing. Lady P knocked on the door.

"Honey what y'all doing?" she asked, laughing.

"They are being gay," I said, chuckling.

Although it sounded as if I was kidding, I said exactly what I was thinking. Two men don't lock up in the bathroom together. I'm sure they figured nobody would suspect foul play was going on, since they were adjacent to the dining room.

Finally, they exited out the restroom. They began setting up in the foyer for a broadcast on Periscope. "Nichol, can I interview you with my audience?" Prophet Ramirez, asked.

"Sure," I replied. I was put on the spot and still trying to seem normal in front of my mother and their spouses.

The three of us squeezed onto the piano bench so that we could be seen on the cell phone screen. Prophet Ramirez logged in with his viewers. He and Apostle Parker were having a theological discussion but were making no sense at all.

They acted so silly on camera, unable to contain themselves because they were "drunk." It was an awkward interview. I was sitting in between the middle of them. Apostle Parker kept laughing as he touched my shoulder, and occasionally placed his hand on my thigh. I felt like lightning was going to strike through the ceiling.

We were getting on the highway heading home that evening. A friend of my mom called as we were on the freeway, and she was made aware that she was on speakerphone. She began to share a testimony how the Lord exposed this man that was pretending to be someone else through Facebook. I began to realize that social media is a common preying field for impostors.

I had so much on my mind riding back home. After all the incidents that had already taken place, I knew these were definite signs to separate myself from Apostle Parker. I felt like a failure in Christ, very **grieved, and disappointed**. I had just attempted to begin my journey of deliverance and this immediately was a hindrance.

I got a message on Facebook while we were halfway home. Another man of God was reaching out to me very concerned. His message read, 'I know you don't know me, but my name is Pastor Roberts. I saw a Periscope video tonight of you with Apostle CJ Parker. It didn't agree with my Spirit, and the Lord was telling me that man is perverted. I see a vision of him messing with young men. Cut ties with him he is trying to sleep with you. God's plan for your life doesn't include him.' I was shocked that God used a total stranger to give me a warning about him. I could not deny that Pastor Roberts had heard from God.

We made it home around 10 PM. I received a call from a lady named Pastor Lyles on the west coast. She was a supporter of my ministry on

Periscope and had been a financial blessing to me before.

"Hey little sister how you doing? I can't talk long, I gotta take my kids to see the firework show. I wanted to call and warn you to be careful with Apostle CJ Parker. I watched the replay video, and I didn't like how he kept touching you. It just wasn't setting right with me," she said.

"I totally understand. I just returned from a weekend revival at his church. Some things transpired that were not of God and I'm trying to pray about how to tell my mom. I appreciate your concern. Thank you," I said.

Since Apostle Parker routinely contacted me through Facebook Messenger, I decided to block him before I went to bed. I didn't have the courage to give a farewell speech. I just wanted what seemed to be a bad dream to end. My mom always would jokingly mention to him how quick I cut people out of my life. “You will never get rid of me,” Apostle Parker said, on many occasions while my mom wasn’t present. In my mind, I kept replaying his voice saying that.

The next morning, I was not in a good mood when I woke up. I was pondering on how to inform my mom of this mess. Apostle Parker had the audacity to call my mom’s phone. Wow this man was persistent. Mom left the house to speak with him in private to relay her concern for my abnormal behavior.

Mom had no idea she was talking to the devil in disguise. He sent me a text message while he was speaking to my mom on the phone. ‘Nichol did you block me?’

‘Yes,’ I typed back.

'I never thought you would do this to me,' he responded. He tried to run a mind game and make me feel guilty.

At that moment, I felt a righteous indignation come over me. In my past, I had an outspoken attitude. I was getting ready to stop suppressing my frustration. I was walking in "false humility," and intimidated by this man's "ministry title." He was no longer going to be allowed to play victim on me. Ephesians 4:26 says, "Be angry and sin not." This "unholy Apostle" had been using his spiritual gifts as a cloak to take advantage of my vulnerability. I walked down the block to call him after they finished talking to get some things off my chest.

"Listen! I cannot be associated with you any longer. Nothing is worth forfeiting my blessings. I want to fulfill my purpose. You shouldn't want to jeopardize your ministry, prophetic gift, or marriage," I said, sincerely stern.

"I never thought you would do this to me. My spiritual gifts always work," Apostle Parker said, arrogantly.

"Wow man you need to repent or you going to hell. I'm gone bye!" I said, hanging up abruptly.

I never spoke to Apostle Parker since that day. I blocked him on every social media site imaginable. Once my mom returned home, I confessed everything in detail to her. Mom wanted to call him back to confront him, but the Holy Spirit led her to refrain from any further contact.

My mom went on Periscope to warn others to beware of "seducing spirits." She mentioned everything except his name. After the broadcast 3 other women sent me a message telling me how Apostle Parker had been enticing them.

A year later, we saw the Pastor who invited Apostle Parker to Toledo to preach on the Breaking News. The one that used the phrase, "Ole stanky ho" over the pulpit was arrested by the FBI for sex trafficking minors and given a life sentence.

I repented unto the Lord for days feeling as if he did not hear me. 1 John 1:9 says, "If we confess our sins He is faithful and just to forgive us and CLEANSE us from all unrighteousness." I had embrace the blood appropriated at Calvary and not let the devil run mind games. I felt so relieved after disconnecting from Apostle Parker. I renounced a plethora of things to evict these illegal demonic principalities. That situation taught me a "valuable lesson." I began fasting three times a week literally for a year.

I realized that sanctification is a process that must be maintained even after liberation.

Encountering this pitfall caused my discernment to become sharper. Moving forward I walked circumspectly. I adopted a lifestyle of holiness through a routine of prayer and fasting. Jesus opened several ministry doors through television as I emerged into a butterfly. I do not claim to be perfect, but I have purpose.

I will not allow myself to be put in that sort of position again by the grace of God. I am so cautious now, I don't even respond to messages from men after a certain hour. Some have tried to test my integrity, but I do not entertain it one bit. Satan assigns people to bring you down and I cannot afford another setback.

Thankfully, I did not have sex with that man but I know the bible says if you look upon someone with lust you already committed adultery in your heart. I have been celibate since I made a commitment to Christ on December 14, 2014. I pray that I continue to remain free from sexual vices. Reading the word of God strengthens the inner man, so when temptations arise we can shun the very appearance of evil. I am a witness that God can make you a new creature if you're willing.

Beloved, believe not every spirit, but try the spirits whether they are of God: because many false prophets are gone out into the world. —1 John 4:1

Nichol Collins

LUST IS ON AN ASSIGNMENT

I have come to the conclusion that several men in church leadership are battling perverted proclivities. I am aware that women are ministers of the gospel, as I am one myself. There are "lipstick lesbians" in ministry (and those who live regular lives), but that's not the topic in this particular book. You must read my story titled, "Church Politics" to hear more details about the ladies.

A lot of male preachers struggle with their sexuality in silence. The devil attacks the character of the Apostolic and Prophetic overseers in an attempt to contaminate spiritual offices. Men carry the seed of reproduction, so societies agenda is to emasculate males. A leaders credibility becomes compromised once he engages in perversion, fornication, and infidelity it takes away credibility. Satan wants to make the church look fraudulent and powerless.

For unto whomsoever much is given, of him shall be much required.

—Luke 12:48 (KJV)

People are already skeptical of preachers due to adulterous scandals on the up-rise. Several leaders have been exposed for decades. I do understand that although these vessels are a man of God, they're still just "a man." Every human being has a sinful nature. It is vital that one does not get comfortable in darkness, but quickly repents if they make a mistake. A man's most vulnerable moment is after he has preached. The adversary wants to detour those designated to bring the Good News to lost souls.

What is disheartening to me is that these Godly figures live double lives. The money that ministry brings into a flourishing congregation has caused some to live in hypocrisy sneaking around on the "Low Down prowl with men." Many anointed men hide behind religion as a mirage. They marry women to cover their inward struggles, or flat out deceive family, friends, and their congregation.

If you were lustful as a single person, marriage won't cure your demons.

A person's obedience to the plan of salvation doesn't eliminate their sinful habits. Deliverance is a marathon, and I truly believe some were never given the tools to be completely set free. Others just didn't try to seek God for wholeness because they chose to straddle the fence.

However, this kind goeth not out, but by prayer and fasting.

—Matthew 7:21 (WBT)

Daniel 11:37 reveals that the Anti-Christ is a homosexual. Marriage between a man and a woman is honorable in the sight of GOD. The devil applauds alternative lifestyles to destroy God's ordinances. Anti means against and Christ means the anointed one, so the enemy is against the anointing!

Most men will give public accolades on social media to make it appear that their marriage is successful. Half of the time they are never home and do all their "dirt" on the road. I'm not saying that a man is gay just because they post nice things about their wives, but often times this is done out of guilt. Flattery is a gateway to deception.

Their wives feel validated and ignore the signs, blinded by a web of lies. Men are aware that women love to be taken care of and money can cause one to go along even after discovering infidelity. Down low preachers are master manipulators, very conniving, and use smooth talking promises to keep you on board. Their charismatic gifts are another enticement. You would never expect a pastor to be involved in such detestable practices.

Witchcraft works with lust, and people control you by your emotions. Perversion is a spirit that has absolutely no boundaries. These leaders prey on young men and become their mentor/spiritual father, which is called grooming. Many young men are seeking their leader's approval, and end up being pimped, robbed, and sabotaged. As influential figures, DL preachers use their charming personalities as bait to seduce those who are vulnerable. Often times, their travel companion is a secret lover or they utilize gay dating apps upon arrival.

The Holy Spirit reveals secrets. If you truly want to know something, ask the Lord to show you exactly what is going on. If you are a Spirit-filled believer God will not allow you to be put to shame. Be ready for what he shows you. I told a few people this and within days the truth came out.

"Not everyone who says to me, 'Lord, Lord, will enter the kingdom of heaven, but the one who does the will of my Father who is in heaven. On that day many will say to me, 'Lord, Lord, did we not prophesy in your name, and cast out demons in your name, and do many mighty works in your name?' And then will I declare to them, 'I never knew you; depart

from me, you workers of lawlessness.
—Matthew 7:21-23 (ESV)

It's impossible for one woman to satisfy a man battling perversion.

BEWARE SIGNS

Today, LGBTQ laws have been passed causing many to feel liberated. Although, there are numerous men who are openly gay, there is a proportion of those having sex with men leading **secret** lives. Do you suspect your boyfriend or husband of being on the (DL) **down low?** Many men in heterosexual relationships are bi-sexual **unbeknownst** to their wives or girlfriends. Some of these men view it like another form of entertainment, or recreation. It is sad to say that some of our young men in college are engaging in homosexual acts as a pledge for fraternities.

African Americans make up only 12 percent of the population in America.

Yet, they account for half of all new reported H.I.V. infections. There have always been men of all races who have had secret sexual lives with men. DL culture has **increased** in recent years, and developed its own modern society.

These guys view the closet as a fearful shell to hide. Black men on the down low typically choose to remain on the DL for a lifetime. Since they don't consider themselves as gay, there is no reason to "come out the closet." A moment of truth is **never** announced.

Most of the black community view homosexuality as shameful and disgusting behavior. Other races are more accepting which lead to fewer double lives, less criticism, and less unprotected sex. So many in this double-lifestyle figure, 'It's easier for me to be discreet about my personal affairs.'

Down low men struggle with their inner demons of acceptance in society. Most men that have been to jail or prison have engaged in homosexual activity whether it was voluntarily or involuntarily. What is referred to as "behind the walls," is defined as keeping quiet about what transpires while incarcerated.

Once an inmate is released, he attempts to adapt back into society. "Pandora's box" has already been opened causing him to crave **unnatural** intimacy. To avoid being labeled derogatory terms such as: "fag," "queer," or "homo," he camouflages his sexuality. Instead of the risk of being seen at gay clubs they surf around on gay dating apps called: Jack'd, Backpage, Grinder, Manhunt, Adam4Adam, Hornet, Surge, Taimi, Scruff, Daddyhunt etc.

Check the history in your computer browser history.

One easy way to check your browser history is to look at the drop-down menu when you type a web address. The recent sites are listed right there. Peradventure, he has deleted the browser history you can open a new browser window as if you want to check something and Press CTRL + H. If you discover anything inappropriate, don't fall for your spouse telling you that it must be your kids. Investigate into your findings further.

The other percentage of DL men have **never** been to jail. But struggling with perversion has plagued them throughout their lifetime. For many, molestation is never disclosed. Unfortunately, being sexually violated in their adolescence opened a demonic doorway that becomes a bad habit. Only 16% of men have documented histories of sexual abuse (by social service agencies, which means it was very serious).

Over the years **the gym** has become the central location for DL men to meet up for sexual activity in the showers or sauna. The idea of creeping around brings an adrenaline rush to hurry up, and climax. They return home acting as if nothing ever happened. Most men have vivid imaginations and are fixated by oral sex. Men have a stronger jawline to stimulate the shaft of a penis while performing oral sex. In several cases DL men like to be anally penetrated. It is considered degrading to their masculinity, but they convince themselves that it's just an act of being freaky.

A "red flag" for any woman dating a down-low man is when he attempts to anally penetrate you with his finger, or penis. A woman's anatomy is enough to pleasure a man because God intended it to be this way. Anything involving anal sex is opening up a desire for strange flesh. A man on the DL may ask you to play with his butthole, which is a red flag also. Another caution is they "always" want to have sex from behind (doggy-style) focusing on your buttocks. Someone in love wants to look directly at you and engage in a kiss while in the heat of passion. If they are only worried about engaging from the rear I would raise a brow.

Don't misconstrue what I am saying, different sexual positions in a marriage are perfectly fine. However, be mindful of the emotional disconnect. Sex toys such as butt plugs, and pornography open doorways to perversion. Signs are often ignored by women in these types of misleading relationships.

Down low men are "homophobic" to take the suspicion off of them. Being gay, is the last thing you would suspect about your man if he always makes **harsh remarks** about homosexuals. Spending much of their time with a male friend and being excessively groomed are dead giveaways. They will talk about this mysterious friend that knows about you. Oddly, you seem to know nothing about them, or only know them by some "fake" name. If you really feel as though something strange is going on, there is probably a reason.

Trust your instinct.

Also, they often prey on overweight or unattractive women to make them feel privileged. The average insecure woman will be so **happy** to have a man that she won't harass a DL dude about some of his inconsistencies and absence. They like beautiful women too because it makes their image look good to society to have a **"trophy piece."**

These men living double lives use women as what is called a "beard," to cover up their tendencies. According to the Centers for Disease Control, one-third of young black men who have sex with men in America are H.I.V. positive. Sadly, ninety percent of that group are unaware of their diagnosis.

They may attempt to bring their male and female partner together as a decoy to bond. However, many that are not as bold will keep them separated. A **lack of intimacy** is something to be concerned about. Men are sexual creatures and will practically sleep with a monstrous looking female. How do you think prostitute's stay in business? Those that have a high sex drive can easily engage in sexual activity a few times in a day. Many use street drugs as a stimulant for arousal. Also poppers, (a slang term) is chemical called isopentyl nitrate is used inhaled to facilitate anal sex by increasing blood flow and relaxing sphincter muscles. This can enhance sexual pleasure in general.

These mysterious DL men will begin to avoid coming to bed in hopes of you being asleep by the time they lay down. Most men are on their phone and talking on social media apps during the wee hours. You can see on Facebook Messenger the last time they were having an active conversation. For example, go to Facebook Messenger as if you're going to send them a message, and it will show you their last time chatting. Messenger is an easy way to converse discreetly because you can archive messages and photos opposed to them being viewed in cell phone text history. Tik tok, Instagram and Snapchat are all ways to find sexual interests by the presentation of their profiles.

Another sign is when a man is not aroused by you wearing lingerie or seducing him. DL men struggle with porn or computer addictions to websites that appease their fantasies while masturbating. If he is asking you to use a dildo (prosthetic penis), anal beads, or to perform a prostrate massage on him.... Run! Also, pay attention to him seeming to have difficulty finding vaginal entrance. He will try to act like he accidentally aimed at your anal cavity by mistake. He may also begin to hint around about penetrating you anally.

Even if the sex between a husband and wife is still frequent, has he become emotionally distant? Has he stopped being vibrant with laughter? Does he seem spacey and preoccupied? Depression can also be a sign of torment resulting from juggling a double-life. DL men get **easily irritated by women** because that really isn't their preference. They feel obligated to stay for the sake of children, reputation, or family.

Physical and verbal abuse is a common behavior because of frustration.

Also, several DL dudes watch gay porn on their phone. They are protective of their phone, and when they fall asleep, the phone is hidden. When they are awake the phone stays in their pocket.

They are manipulative and use excessive compliments to keep you fooled. Often it is difficult to believe the signs because DL men are always telling a woman how much they love her. This can be a guilt tactic and manipulation when it's an overkill. When he does not initiate sex or doesn't desire it as often he has a new "lust interest."

A WOMAN'S INTUITION IS HER COMPASS, SO DON'T IGNORE THE SIGNS!!

Some DL men shave their body hair, especially their pubic area. Their wardrobe drastically changes to metrosexual clothing. They get their eyebrows cleaned up where it looks neat, but not necessarily feminine. Have you ever caught him taking a photo of himself naked? A beard is even an unspoken silence that you are on the DL. Not every man with a beard is bisexual, but it is a secret sign amongst that community. These geisha girl up-do's, man bun styles are another way they tap into their feminine side.

The thought of a transsexual looking like a woman, but possessing male genitalia captivates DL men. The term "chicks with d*ck*" is an online marketing phrase for men with fetishes. Erosguide.com is a website that shows you ads for transsexual prostitutes. The lustful appetite of human nature is willing to venture into dark dimensions of sexual perversion. The mindset of a DL man thinks he is not committing homosexual acts since the transsexual has breast implants. They travel to tranny parties where DL men and tranny's penetrate each other, which is a term called "flip flopping."

Men who live on the down-low often exhibit narcissistic traits, using gaslighting and manipulation to maintain control over their partners. They thrive on secrecy and deception, making their relationships a battleground of confusion and emotional turmoil.

A down-low man will do whatever it takes to protect his double life, including distorting reality, shifting blame, and making his partner question her own perceptions. He'll deny obvious red flags, twist conversations, and make her feel like she's overreacting, all while continuing his deception. This kind of man craves control, not just over his image but over the emotions and thoughts of the woman he's stringing along.

Many times, he's also a **mama's boy**, raised to believe he can do no wrong. His mother often enables his behavior, dismissing any concerns and reinforcing the idea that he's above accountability. To her, he's perfect—so when his partner starts noticing inconsistencies, she's met with resistance from both him and his family.

The result? A woman left in **emotional chaos**, constantly questioning herself, feeling disoriented, drained, and unsure of what's real. She may even start blaming herself, wondering if she's imagining things or being too harsh. This is exactly what he wants—because as long as she's doubting herself, she's less likely to expose the truth.

Escaping this cycle requires **clarity, self-trust, and the courage to walk away** from the manipulation. A woman must recognize that the problem isn't her intuition—it's the deception designed to make her doubt it.

The entertainment industry has accepted bi-sexual behaviors as normal. It's almost like heterosexual individuals are the odd balls out of the bunch. There will be an offer made that most cannot refuse to "turn out" actors and music artists into this underground freak fest. It has spilled over into the athletic arena as well. This keeps people from disclosing secrets in these underground societies.

Women become like a puppet on a string. Most things start off well to get you hooked. Once the pattern changes you are living in the past. "Oh, how I wish things were the way they used to be," will be your favorite line rehearsed in your mind. Intercourse links many together mentally, emotionally, and physically. Sex outside of marriage causes a person to become entangled with the personality traits of that individual. The negative effect of fornication can also be used for the devil's advantage.

For this sort are they which creep into houses, and lead captive silly women laden in sins, led away with divers lusts. Ever learning, and never able to come to the knowledge of the truth.

—2 Timothy 3:6-7 (KJV)

Sadly, I must emphasize the importance of not being naive when it comes to your companion's close relationship with a male pastor. We have seen, time and again, headlines exposing deceased leaders who were involved in inappropriate relationships with their so-called "spiritual sons."

In my opinion, it is out of order for a married man to be assigned to travel out of town with the pastor. His first priority should be his wife, not the leader. Surely, there must be someone single who can assist with itinerant ministry. Even then, you never truly know what is transpiring behind closed doors.

I personally know of two incidents within the church circuit that expose this hidden reality. One woman I knew attended a prominent ministry led by a well-known gospel artist and preacher. Later, it was revealed that her husband was secretly involved with the bishop. Beforehand, when she shared some concerns with me, I immediately sensed that something was unnatural. One night, after taking my advice and placing a GPS tracker on his car, she was hysterical. She merged me on the line as everything unraveled—she had tracked him to a location where the bishop was fully "queening out," speaking in an openly effeminate manner.

In another case, a first lady had long harbored suspicions about her husband. One day, while cleaning, she kept hearing a text alert. Tracing the sound, she discovered an alternate phone hidden deep in the couch cushions. Her husband had been concealing another device—one that revealed his so-called "best friend," an openly gay man, was actually his lover. Devastated, she reached out to me. She admitted that she had always felt uneasy about their close friendship but dismissed it because their families had raised them as cousins. What didn't come out in the wash eventually came out in the rinse.

We must not blindly follow our hearts. That dangerous myth has misled many into ignoring red flags that could have prevented heartbreak and betrayal.

I did not write this book to be sexually graphic or to sensationalize these issues. I wrote it to **warn and enlighten** women about the realities that many refuse to acknowledge. The truth is, you cannot underestimate these men or the things they engage in behind the scenes. I pray that this message reaches someone in time to prevent unnecessary disaster.

God bless!

Nichol Collins

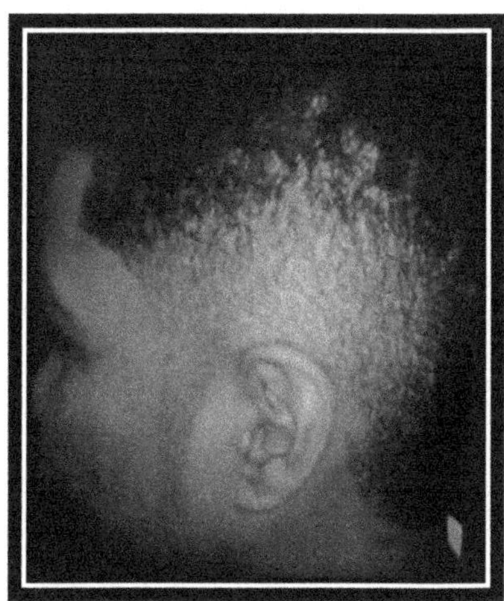

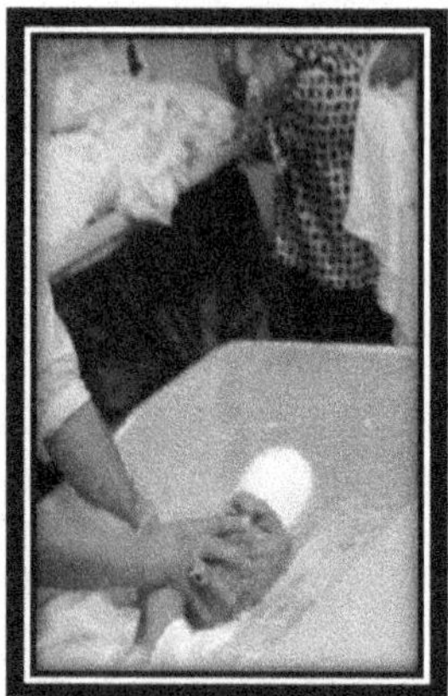

Acts 2:38

Caterpillar2Butterfly

Contact or Shop @Globeshakers.com

www.ingramcontent.com/pod-product-compliance
Lightning Source LLC
Chambersburg PA
CBHW032103080426
42733CB00006B/390

9780999754535